EVERYTHING THAT YOU NEED TO KNOW ABOUT OUR FISHY FRIENDS

Animal Book Age 5
Children's Animal Books

Baby Professor
EDUCATION KIDS

Speedy Publishing LLC
40 E. Main St. #1156
Newark, DE 19711
www.speedypublishing.com
Copyright 2017

In this book, we're going to cover interesting facts about fish. So, let's get right to it!

There are over 30,000 species of fish. They are vertebrate animals that live underwater. They come in all different sizes, shapes, and colors. Even though they breathe oxygen to live, they don't have to come up to the surface for air. Their gills take the oxygen from the water.

Scientists think that fish appeared on Earth around 500 million years ago. At that time, there were lots of soft-bodied creatures like jellyfish living underwater. Jellyfish aren't fish, even though they have "fish" in their name. Fish were the first creatures to have skeletons on their insides as well as scales and spines on their outsides.

WHAT MAKES A FISH A TRUE FISH?

Most fish are cold-blooded animals that live underwater. Also, for the most part, fish have skeletons, gills, and fins. So, even though a crocodile is cold-blooded and has a skeleton, it isn't a fish because it doesn't have gills or fins.

A shark is a very large fish because it has a skeleton made of cartilage, fins, and gills. Some sharks are partly warm-blooded but that's unusual for most fish. A jellyfish isn't a fish because it doesn't have a skeleton, gills, or fins.

TYPES OF FISH

There are three main groups of fish. The three types are:

Jawless fish—an example is an eel

Cartilaginous fish—an example is a shark

Bony fish—an example is a trout

HOW DO FISH BREATHE?

Whales and dolphins may look like big fish but they are mammals instead. They can't breathe underwater like fish can. They have to come up to the surface for oxygen. Fish need oxygen to live too. However, they breathe in water instead of air. They get oxygen from water and let out carbon dioxide, just like we do with air.

WHERE DO FISH LIVE?

Some fish live in freshwater. Other types live in saltwater. You'll find fish in every different kind of waterway on Earth. Some fish live on the water's surface, some live midway down, and some live so deep down there's no light.

WHAT DO FISH EAT?

Many types of fish eat algae or under-water plants of different types. Some types of fish just open their mouths wide and then filter out food from the water that flows through their mouths. Some fish eat other fish. Fish that eat other fish hunt in different ways. For example, sharks directly attack their prey. Other types of fish hide under the sand or among rocks to make a sneak attack.

WHAT IS A GROUP OF FISH CALLED?

When you use the word "school" you think of a building where you learn, but a group of fish is also called a school. Fish travel in numbers so they are harder to catch. When they travel in an organized way, they are in a school. If they are just grouped together in different directions then they are in a shoal.

A SCHOOL OF BLUESTRIPE SNAPPER

FISH AS PETS

Certain types of small fish make great pets. Fish are not hard to take care of, but they do need to be in water that is right for them, either soft acidic water or hard alkaline water. Some need salt and some don't.

They need the proper kind of daily food as well as the proper type of aquarium. Also, it's important to keep their aquarium clean and at the right type of water temperature. Many types of fish are very colorful and really fun to watch.

FASTEST, LONGEST, HEAVIEST, SHORTEST FISH

Sailfish can swim over 60 miles per hour. They are the fastest.

Whale sharks measure 40 feet or more long. They are the longest.

Ocean sunfish weigh 5,000 pounds. They are the heaviest.

SUNFISH

DWARF GOBY

Dwarf goby are only 9 millimeters in length. They are the shortest. Because they are so small, they make good aquarium pets.

Fish are all so different from each other! Here are some interesting types in alphabetical order.

FLYING FISH

Did you know there are some fish that can fly? Flying fish can use their fins as "wings." They can jump away from other fish that are trying to eat them. They jump high out of the water and glide on the air. They can go as high as 4 feet over the water surface and glide for over 600 feet.

Once a flying fish gets close to the water again, it can flap its tail and move slowly along without going underwater completely. Flying fish get up to 18 inches long and they live in warm ocean waters around the world.

FROGFISH

Frogfish live in oceans worldwide. They are sometimes very difficult to see underwater because they disguise themselves. They have unique bumps and spines that they use to make themselves look like underwater sponges. Frogfish are a type of anglerfish.

ANGLERFISH

nglerfish are known for catching other fish with their own version of a "fishing pole" and "bait." They have a special fin with a piece that looks like a shrimp on the end of it. Fish think it's a real shrimp and when they go after it, the frogfish grab them up to eat them.

GROUPER

Groupers can get up to 10 feet long and they can weigh over 1,000 pounds. They can be found in the Indian and Pacific Oceans. Groupers are like giant vacuum cleaners. When they open their mouths, the suction is so strong they can inhale fish!

Groupers can change the color of their skin to hide from other fish that might eat them. They can sometimes change their skin to show different color patterns like spots and splotches.

They use these changes to blend in with the coral where they live. These big fish travel in groups with one male and several females. If the male fish dies, one of the females can become a male and lead the group!

HALIBUT

Halibut are among the largest fish of the sea. Halibut that weigh more than 100 pounds are called "whales." Those that weigh less than 20 pounds are called "chickens."

Halibut is a very popular food. It has a sweet flavor and very flaky meat. They are found in the North Atlantic Ocean, North Pacific Ocean, and the Bering Sea.

JOHN DORY FISH

This very strange-looking fish has an oval-shaped body that's flat and a spiny head. It has a large, dark spot on its side. This eyespot is used to confuse other fish it wants to eat and to scare off fish that want to eat it. It's a popular source of food and is used for fish and chips.

LIONFISH

Lionfish have colorful stripes and long, feathery fins. Even though their spines are venomous, they are popular aquarium fish. They use their spines to defend themselves against other fish.

They were accidentally introduced to the east coast of the United States and are killing lots of other fish that are native to those waters. A sting from a lionfish is very painful to humans.

MORAY EEL

E els don't look like fish but they are fish. Moray eels can get over 9 feet long and they look something like snakes swimming in the water. They can be found hiding in crevices of rocks so that other fish don't eat them.

SEAHORSE

There are 47 different species of seahorses and 14 of them were recently discovered. Some of these unique creatures have heads shaped like horses and this is where they got their name. Seahorses don't have teeth and they don't have stomachs so they have to eat all the time to stay alive.

They latch onto sea grasses and coral with their curved tails and suck in plankton and small brine shrimp. They can eat up to 3,000 brine shrimp every day. The females deposit their eggs inside the males and the males give birth to the tiny live seahorses.

SUNFISH

Even though a sunfish grows to a huge size, it looks like it's just the head of a fish instead of a whole fish. The sunfish's back fin never grows. Instead, it folds on top of itself and creates a "rudder" at the back of the fish that it uses to steer in the water.

TANG

Tangs come in colors of bright yellow and blue. They like to live in shallow coral reefs where they can hide from fish that eat them. They are named for the scalpel at the base of their tails, which is called a tang.

YELLOW TANG

They use this scalpel to attach them-selves to coral or to fight off predators, which are the fish that want to eat them. They also use it to clean up turtles by scraping the algae off their backs.

Awesome! Now you know a lot more about all different kinds of fish. You can find more Animal books from Baby Professor by searching the website of your favorite book retailer.

Visit
BABY PROFESSOR
EDUCATION KIDS
www.BabyProfessorBooks.com
to download Free Baby Professor eBooks
and view our catalog of new and exciting
Children's Books